The King's Cape

by Jean Groce

ISBN 0-15-313849-1

Ordering Options
ISBN 0-15-313991-9 (Grade 1 Collection)
ISBN 0-15-314058-5 (package of 5)

 2 3 4 5 6 7 8 9 10 026 99

One day three men were working
in the King's garden. They found an
old trunk and lifted it out of the
ground. Then the men scrubbed the
old trunk, and when they were done,
one of them said, "Let's take it to the
King!" This is just what they did.

When the King opened the trunk, he was very surprised. "Look at this," he shouted. "What a cape! It shines just like the sun. I almost have to close my eyes!"

2

The King put on the cape. Then he walked all over town saying, "Look at me! I shine like the sun! Who could want the sun when I shine like this?"

Everybody looked at the King. "We do not want the sun," they said. "The sun never shined like our King!"

Up in the sky,
the sun saw this
and was not happy.
"They think they do not
want me, so I'll go away!"
This is just what the sun did.

4

The next morning, the sun did
not come up. It was night all day long.
The King put on his cape, but it did
not shine in the night.

"Look!" everybody said. "It is night all day! What fun! We will not have to get up in the morning. And here is the best part. We will not have to work! We can just play and play all day!"

It was always night. Soon, having night all day was not fun. No one worked and no one played.

"This is not good," everybody whispered.

At last they went to see the King.

"Our eyes can't see in the night. We can't do our work. What will we do?"

"I don't shine like the sun after all," the King said. "I now know we have to have the sun. I will go and ask the sun to shine again."

8

So the King went off to see the
sun. He walked for days. He climbed
up hill after hill. He climbed up as
high as he could go.

At last the King came to some
steps. When he climbed them,
the King was at the top of
the world! Here the
King found the sun.

"Sun!" said the King. "At last I've found you. Could you shine for us once again?"

"Why?" asked the sun. "You said you didn't want me. You think you shine like I do. You make day come."

10

"No," said the King, shaking his head. "My cape shines only when you shine. Only you are the sun. I'll never again say you are not wanted."

The sun was happy now. It started to shine.

So once more the sun came up
every day. Everybody was glad.

The King put the shining cape
back into the trunk. "I'll never put it on
again," he said.

And he didn't.

TAKE-HOME BOOK
All Smiles
Use with "Henry and Mudge in the Green Time."